Written and Illustrated by Lauren Holbrook

Hebrews 4:12
"For the word of God is living and active, sharper than any two-edged sword, piercing to the division of soul and of spirit, of joints and of marrow, and discerning the thoughts and intentions of the heart."

Copyright © 2020 by Lauren Holbrook
All rights reserved. This book or any portion thereof
may not be reproduced or used in any manner whatsoever
without the express written permission of the publisher
except for the use of brief quotations in a book review.

First Printing, 2020

ISBN 978-0-578-60553-1

Laurel Crown Publishing

www.thecrybook.com

Psalms 139:17-18
"How precious are your thoughts of me, oh God! How vast is the sum of them! If I were to count them, they would number more than the grains of sand."

Luke 12:6-7
"Are not five sparrows sold for two pennies? And not one of them is forgotten before God. Why, even the hairs on your head are all numbered. Fear not; you are more value than many sparrows."

Romans 8:38-39
"For I am convinced that neither death nor life, nor angels nor principalities nor powers, nor things present nor things to come, nor height nor depth, nor any other created thing, shall be able to separate us from the love of God which is in Christ Jesus our Lord."

Ephesians 6:12
"For our fight is not against flesh and blood, but against the rulers, against the authorities, against the powers of this dark world and against the spiritual forces of evil in the heavenly realms."

Psalms 8:3-9
"When I considered your heavens, the work of your fingers, the moon and the stars, which you have set in place; What is man, that you take thought of him? And the son of man, that you would care for him? Yet you have made him a little lower than God, and you have crown him with glory and honor! You have made him ruler of the works of your hands; you have put all things under his feet…Oh Lord our Lord, how majestic is your name in all the earth!"

Life is precious. Before the Lord God hung the stars and the planets in the galaxy, before He harnessed the seas and oceans, before He commanded the wind, He knew every child that ever has been and ever will be. He knew them by name. And He loves them with a love that cannot be contained by any perimeter, and they will never be separated from Him.

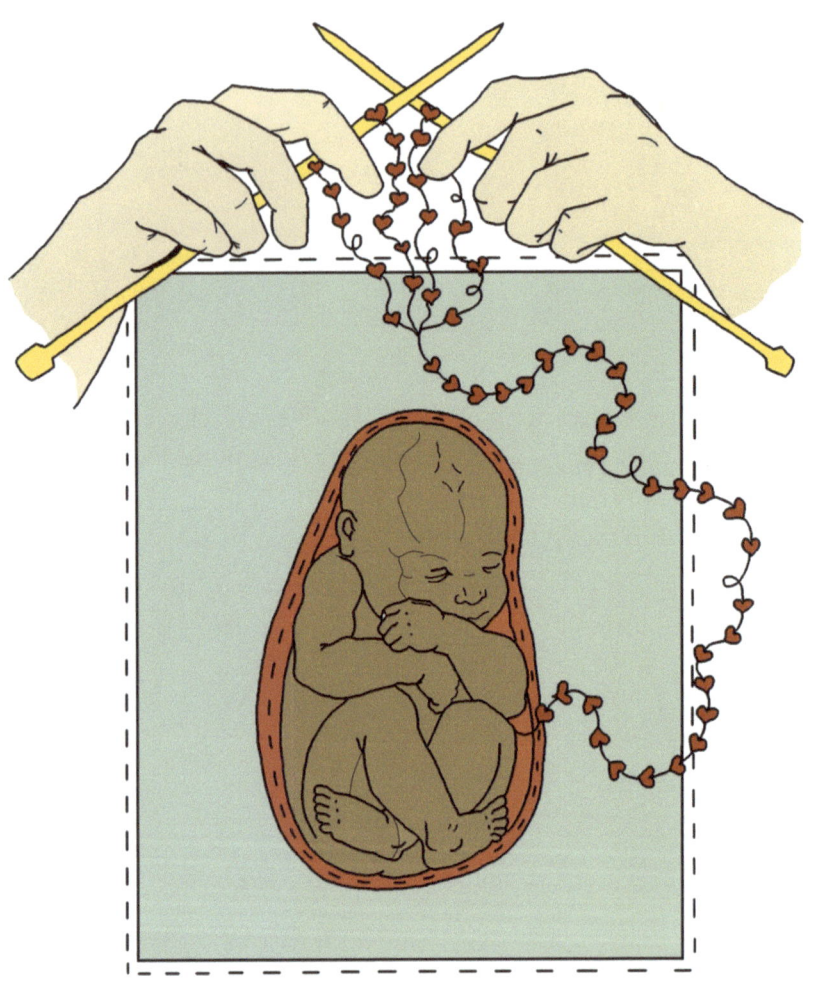

Psalms 139:13-16
"For you created my inmost being; you knit me together in my mother's womb. I praise you because I am fearfully and wonderfully made; your works are wonderful, I know that full well. My frame was not hidden from you when I was made in the secret place, when I was woven together in the depths of the earth. Your eyes saw my unformed body; all the days ordained for me were written in your book
before one of them came to be."

From a hidden place, every part of every baby is knit and woven together with the same power that created the heavens and the earth. The miracle of life is made whole in a tiny human! Can you see the love that God has poured into them? Every detail, every tiny, intricate part of them is loved and wanted.

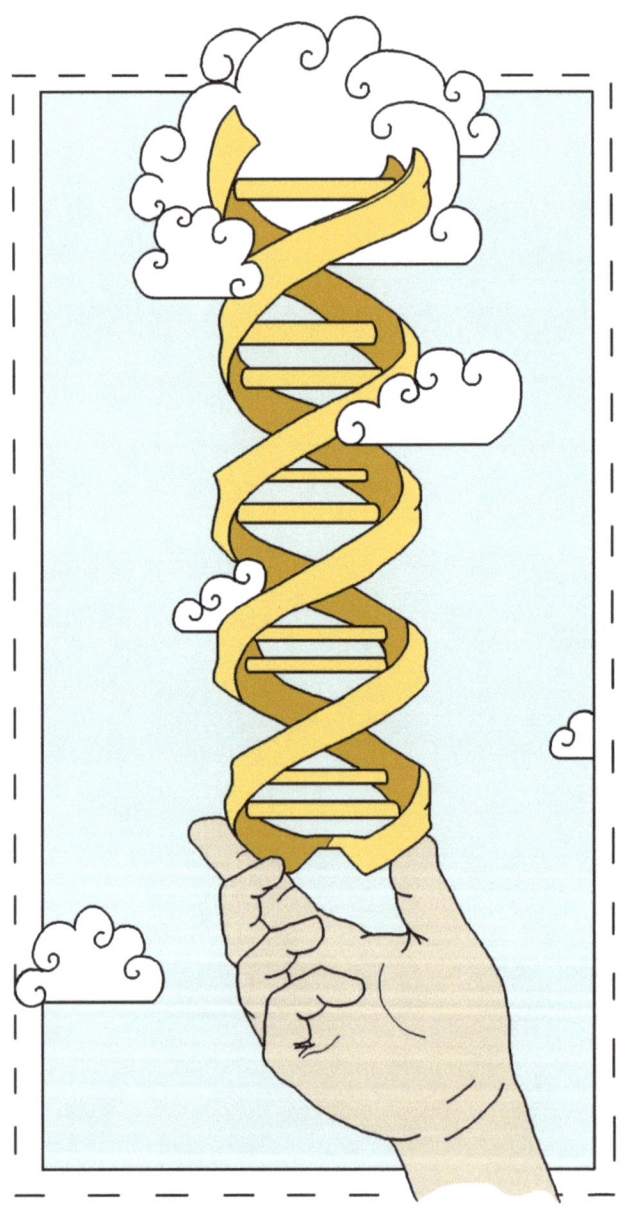

Psalms 139:14
"I praise you because I am fearfully and wonderfully made; your works are wonderful, I know that full well."

From the very moment they were conceived, each baby has a unique set of DNA that has never been seen before nor will ever be repeated again. They are fully human from the second God creates them. 22 days from that moment, the baby has a heart beat. Less than a month old, the baby has eyes and ears and a respiratory system. As they grow, the wonders continue! When they are 20 weeks old, they can kick and turn, and their vocal chords are fully formed. Can you see the miracle that they are? Can you see the incredible work of brilliance that they are? God, in all His unchallenged wisdom, has made them perfectly.

Isaiah 49:15
"Can a mother forget her nursing child, and have no compassion on the son of her womb? Though she may forget, I will not forget you!"

But there is a horrific war that is being waged against these tiny, wonderful human beings.
There is an Enemy who plans for their destruction. He has lied and said their lives have no worth. He has lied and said that babies are something to despise. He has lied and said it would be better if they weren't here.
Some have believed him.
Some men and women want to end those precious lives before they have hardly begun.
They call it abortion, the ending of a baby's life.
What should cause a heart to feel anguish and horror, some cry out in celebration, "Victory!"
And there are others still who have closed their ears, refusing to hear the cries of the innocent and helpless.
And even in this, the Lord's compassion cannot be removed. He has not, and will never stop, loving those who He has made .

Job 17:7
"My eyes have grown dim with grief; my whole frame is but a shadow."

The babies,
those tiny miracles,
have reached for their mothers
and fathers,
but they were abandoned.
Their hands were not held.
Their tears were not dried.
Their cries were not answered.

Psalm 121:1
"I lift my eyes up to the mountains- where does my help come from? My help comes from the Lord, the Maker of heavens and earth."

And so the babies have cried out to the Lord God Almighty. The one who hung the stars and planets in the galaxy, who harnessed the seas and oceans, and commanded the wind. The one who knows every child that ever has been and ever will be. The one who knows them by name. The one who loves them with a love that cannot be contained by any perimeter, and who's love will never be seperated from them.

Psalm 91:4
"He will cover you with His feathers, and under His wings you will find refuge; His faithfulness will be your shield and protection."

And He who created the world and all that is
within it, is answering.
He has heard their cries.
He is coming to their rescue.

Proverbs 24:11-12
"Rescue those who are unjustly sentenced to death; don't stand back and let them die. Don't try to disclaim responsibility to say you didn't know about it."

And He is sending you.
He has made an army of the strongest people on earth, His people. He has given you a voice to sound a battle cry that will shake this world as we rise up to protect and defend the most innocent and helpless of God's creations. Open your ears to hear! Open your eyes to see! And be ready for what God is calling you to do next. For God has assigned each one of us with different responsibilities, and you are essential and irreplaceable in sounding
The Cry.

At the moment of conception, there are flashes of light, or fireworks. (1)

All human chromosomes are present at fertilization. (4)

In that fraction of a second when the chromosomes form pairs, the sex of the new child will be determined, hereditary characteristics received from each parent will be set, and a new life will have begun. (2)

A baby's heart beat starts at 22 days old. (3) The heart beats the baby's own blood, often a different blood type than their mothers. (4)

Brain waves are detectable by 6 weeks old. (4)

The baby is kicking and swimming by 7 weeks old. (4)

By 8 weeks old, every organ is in place; bones and fingerprints begin to form. (4)

The baby can turn their head and frown by the time they are 10 weeks old. (4)

The baby can have dream sleep (REM) by the time they are 17 weeks old. (4)

As of 2016, 88% of all abortions happen during the first trimester. (5)

In the United States, approximately 800,000 abortions per year are performed in the first trimester of pregnancy. Nearly 100,000 abortions per year are performed in the second and third trimester. (6)

1. Fellman, Megan. "Stunning Zinc Fireworks When Egg Meets Sperm." Northwestern, Northwestern University, Dec 15, 2014, https://news.northwestern.edu/stories/2014/12/stunning-zinc-fireworks-when-egg-meets-sperm.
2. Kaluger, G., and Kaluger, M., Human Development: The Span of Life, page 28-29, The C.V. Mosby Co., 1974.
3. Green, Emma. "When Does A Baby's Heart Begin To Beat." PregWorld, May 14, 2017, https://www.pregworld.org/when-does-a-babys-heart-begin-to-beat/.
4. "The Basics A Compilation Of Recent And Noteworthy Information On The Abortion Issue." National Right to Life Educational Foundation, National Rights to Life Educational Foundation, accessed September 26, 2019, http://www.nrlc.org/uploads/factsheets/FS02TheBasics.pdf.
5. "U.S. Abortion Statistics. Facts and Figures relating to the Frequency of Abortions in the United State." Abort73.com, accessed Jan 17, 2020, https://www.abort73.com/abortion_facts/us_abortion_statistics/.
6. "Abortion Facts." AbortionNo, accessed Jan 21, 2020, https://www.abortionno.org/abortion-facts/.

www.ingramcontent.com/pod-product-compliance
Lightning Source LLC
Chambersburg PA
CBHW041745040426
42444CB00001B/42